We Can Be Responsible!

WE HELP CLEAN UP

By Lynda Arnéz

Gareth Stevens PUBLISHING

Please visit our website, www.garethstevens.com. For a free color catalog of all our high-quality books, call toll free 1-800-542-2595 or fax 1-877-542-2596.

Cataloging-in-Publication Data

Names: Arnéz, Lynda.
Title: We help clean up! / Lynda Arnéz.
Description: New York : Gareth Stevens Publishing, 2020. | Series: We can be responsible!
Identifiers: ISBN 9781538239117 (pbk.) | ISBN 9781538239131 (library bound) | ISBN 9781538239124 (6 pack)
Subjects: LCSH: Cleaning–Juvenile literature. | Housekeeping–Juvenile literature. | Chores–Juvenile literature.
Classification: LCC TX324.A76 2019 | DDC 648'.5–dc23

First Edition

Published in 2020 by
Gareth Stevens Publishing
111 East 14th Street, Suite 349
New York, NY 10003

Editor: Kristen Nelson
Designer: Sarah Liddell

Photo credits: Cover, p. 1 Lopolo/Shutterstock.com; p. 5 Yuganov Konstantin/Shutterstock.com; p. 7 Dmitri Ma/Shutterstock.com; p. SPY_studio/Shutterstock.com; p. 11 Africa Studio/Shutterstock.com; p. 13 Maria Evseyeva/Shutterstock.com; pp. 15, 24 (broom) Olga Evans/Shutterstock.com; p. 17 Studio Romantic/Shutterstock.com; pp. 19, 24 (rake) Fuse/Corbis/Getty Images; p. 21 Suzanne Tucker/Shutterstock.com; p. 23 Rawpixel.com/Shutterstock.com.

Printed in the United States of America

CPSIA compliance information: Batch #CS19GS: For further information contact Gareth Stevens, New York, New York at 1-800-542-2595.

Contents

It is time to clean up! What should we do to help?

There are
toys everywhere!

Jack puts his toys in the toy box.

Morgan puts dirty clothes in the washer.

Gabby cleans up
her room.
She makes her bed!

Paul sweeps.
He uses a broom.

Mae and her sister wash the floor.

We can help outside, too.
Thomas rakes leaves.

My older brother mows the lawn.
It makes the grass short!

You can help clean up!
What will you do?

Words to Know

broom

rake

Index